The Nature Kid's Guide to SWANS

DAVID ANDERSON

LP Media Inc. Publishing
Text copyright © 2026 by LP Media Inc.
All rights reserved.

For information address LP Media Inc. Publishing,
30012 Variolite St NW, Princeton MN 55371
www.lpmedia.org

Publication Data

Swans
The Nature Kid's Guide to Swans — First edition.

Summary: "Learn all about Swans, the Nature Kid Way"
— Provided by publisher.

ISBN: 979-8-89818-217-5

[1. Swans – Non-Fiction] I. Title.

Title: The Nature Kid's Guide to Swans

CONTENTS

SERENE SHORES

Some swans return to the exact same lake every single year for their whole life!

Splash! A white swan lands softly on a quiet lake.

Swans are big, graceful birds. They live on lakes, ponds, and slow rivers. Calm water with lots of plants nearby is their favorite spot.

A swan's home needs fresh water and food. Tall reeds and grasses grow at the water's edge, giving swans a safe place to hide and rest. Some swans build nests as wide as a car tire right among these plants.

Other swans live near the sea, too. They pick bays and marshes with still water. Anywhere calm and green with lots of water can become a swan's home.

SWAN SPOTS

Mute swans have yellow or orange on their bills; trumpeter swans have all black bills.

6

Honk! A black swan glides across a pond in Australia.

Swans live on every continent except Africa and Antarctica. White swans glide across lakes in Europe and North America. Black swans call Australia home.

Some swans like cold places. Tundra swans fly to the far north in summer, where the sun barely sets. Whooper swans live in icy parts of Europe and Asia.

Other swans stay in warmer spots year-round. Black-necked swans live in South America. Each kind of swan has its own favorite place to call home.

SUPER SIZED
FUN FACT!
The smallest swan, the coscoroba, weighs about 10 pounds — still bigger than a goose!

Whoosh! A trumpeter swan spreads its giant wings wide.

Trumpeter swans are the biggest **waterfowl** in the world. They can weigh 25 to 30 pounds. That is as heavy as a large dog!

A swan's wings stretch very wide. From tip to tip, they can reach eight feet across. That is wider than most grown-ups are tall.

Swans stand about three to four feet high. A first grader could look one right in the eye! Even the smallest swan is bigger than most ducks and geese.

BUILT BEAUTIFUL

Swans have around 25,000 feathers — more than almost any other bird!

Swish! A swan dips its long, curving neck under the water.

A swan's neck is very long and has many bones. It has more neck bones than a giraffe! All those bones help the swan bend and twist to reach food deep below.

Swans have big, flat feet with skin between their toes. These **webbed** feet work like paddles, pushing the swan smoothly through the water with each kick.

A swan's feathers are thick and tightly packed. They fit close together to keep cold water out. Under those feathers is soft, warm down that traps heat like a cozy blanket.

SHARP SENSES

Shh! A tundra swan hears a sharp snap in the tall grass.

Swans can see very well, even far away. Their eyes sit on the sides of their head, letting them watch for danger in almost every direction at once.

Swans hear well, too. They can pick up soft sounds from far off. A twig snapping nearby will wake a sleeping swan right away.

Swans also feel with their bills. The tips of their beaks can sense food hidden under water. They use this special touch to find plants buried in the mud.

WING WHACK

Thwack! A mute swan flaps its powerful wings. Watch out!

Mute swans are not shy about fighting back. When a threat gets too close, a swan puffs up its feathers. It raises its wings high and hisses loud.

A swan's wings are very strong. One hard hit can bruise or even break bones! Even big animals like dogs and foxes learn to stay away.

Swans also bite with their tough bills. They pinch hard to scare off trouble. Most animals learn quickly that a swan is not worth the fight.

Swans will chase away deer, dogs, and even people who get too close to their nest!

DIP DOWN

Swans swallow small stones called grit to help grind up food in their belly!

Glug! A swan tips upside down to grab plants below.

Swans eat mostly plants that grow in or near the water. They munch on roots, stems, and leaves. Some swans eat grass and grain on land, too.

To eat underwater plants, a swan tips its body forward. Its tail goes up and its head dips down. This is called upending. The swan's long neck reaches all the way to the bottom.

Swans also eat small bugs, snails, and worms. They find these tiny treats in the water and mud. One hungry swan can eat about eight pounds of food in a single day!

HONK HELLO

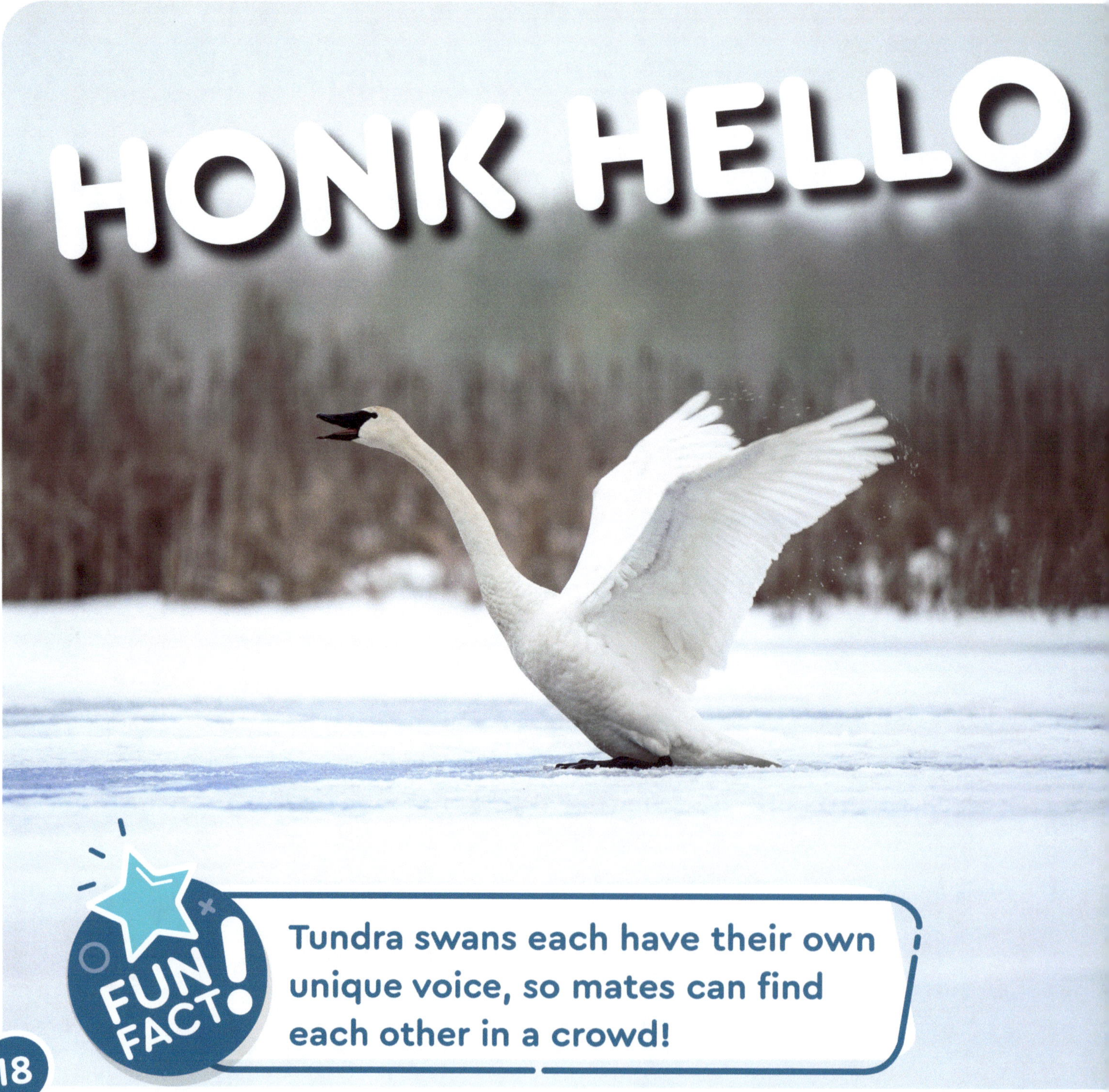

FUN FACT!

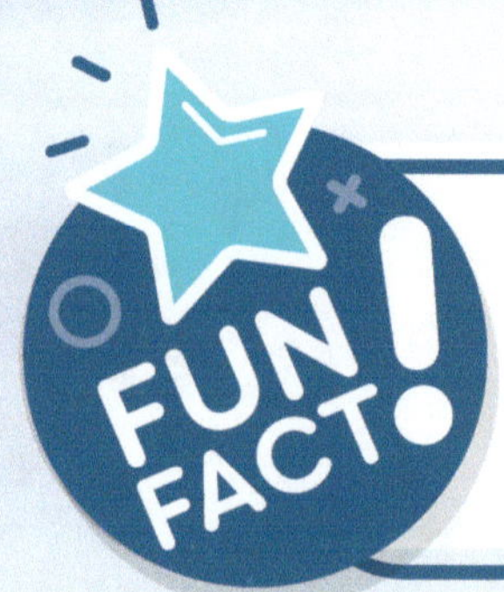

Tundra swans each have their own unique voice, so mates can find each other in a crowd!

Toot! A trumpeter swan blasts its call across the frozen pond.

Each kind of swan makes its own sounds. Trumpeter swans have loud, deep calls like a horn. You can hear them from more than a mile away!

Mute swans are not really mute at all. They make soft grunts, snorts, and low whistles. Their wings also make a humming sound in flight that you can hear from far away.

Swans talk with their bodies, too. A head bob can say hello. If a swan's wings are held high and its neck is stretched out — that means go away!

SNEAKY STALKERS

20

Watch! A swan scans the shore, always looking out for danger.

Adult swans are big and tough. Not many animals dare to hunt them. But foxes, coyotes, and raccoons may sneak up on nesting swans when they least expect it.

Eagles and large owls can attack from above. These birds swoop down fast. Swans on the ground cannot always get away in time.

Baby swans face the most danger. Snapping turtles grab them from below. Hawks, mink, and big fish hunt them, too. That is why swan parents stay so close to their young.

FAST FLIGHT

FUN
FACT!
A scared swan can go from sitting still to full flight speed in just a few seconds!

Flap! A whooper swan races across the water to escape.

When danger comes, a swan runs across the water to take off. Its big feet slap the surface hard. It pumps its huge wings until it lifts into the air.

Once flying, swans are very fast. They can zoom up to 60 miles per hour! Most predators cannot keep up with a swan in the sky.

On water, swans swim away quickly. They tuck their babies close and paddle hard. If they must, they will dive under the surface to hide. Speed keeps swans safe.

GRACEFUL GLIDERS

24

Whirr! A swan's wings beat fast as it flies over the tall trees.

On water, swans look like they float without effort. But under the surface, their webbed feet paddle in circles. It looks easy, but those feet are always working hard.

In the air, swans fly in a V shape with their flock. Each bird rides the wind from the one ahead, saving energy on long trips.

On land, swans waddle slowly. Their legs are set far back on their bodies, making walking tricky. That is why water and sky are their favorite places to be!

DAY DRIFT

Swans love bath time! They splash, roll, and dunk their heads to get squeaky clean.

Ruffle! A black swan shakes its feathers and settles down to rest.

Swans spend a big part of each day eating. They feed in the morning and again before dark. In between, they rest and preen their feathers.

Preening means cleaning and fixing feathers. Swans rub oil from a gland near their tail onto each feather. This keeps their coat shiny and waterproof so they stay warm and dry.

At night, swans sleep on the water or near the shore. They tuck one leg up and rest their head on their back. They even nap with one eye open to stay safe!

FLOCK FUN

A big winter group of tundra swans can have over 10,000 birds splashing together!

Splish splash! A huge group of swans fills the winter lake.

Swans are social birds. Many kinds gather in large groups during winter. A group of swans on water is called a **bevy**.

During the cold months, swans from many families come together. Young swans and old swans share the same lake. The large group keeps them safe and warm.

Swans in a group watch out for each other. If one swan spots danger, it calls out loud. The whole flock can take off together in seconds, leaving trouble behind.

DANCE DATE

FUN FACT!
When two mute swans face each other, their curved necks make a perfect heart shape!

Swoosh! Two swans bow and dip their heads face to face.

When swans find a mate, they do a special dance. The two birds face each other and bob their heads. They dip their necks and touch bills gently.

Most swans pair up for life. That means they stay with the same partner for many years. If one swan is lost, the other may find a new mate after a while.

Before nesting, the pair builds a big mound of sticks and plants. The female lines it with soft down from her chest. Some nests can be six feet wide — as big as a bathtub!

CUTE CYGNETS

Crack! A fuzzy baby swan pokes its way out of the egg.

Baby swans are called **cygnets**. A mother swan lays four to eight eggs in her big nest. She sits on them for about five weeks to keep them warm.

When cygnets hatch, they are covered in soft gray or white fluff. They can walk and swim on their very first day! Within hours, they follow their mother right to the water.

Cygnets grow fast. Their fluffy down turns into real feathers in just a few weeks. By fall, they are almost as big as their parents and ready to fly.

PROUD PARENTS

Peep! A mother swan glides across the lake with four tiny cygnets paddling close behind.

Both swan parents take care of their young. The father watches for danger while the mother leads the cygnets to food. They work as a team all day long.

Swan parents teach their babies how to find food. They lead them to spots with lots of plants. Cygnets watch closely and copy what their parents do.

The family stays together for many months. Parents chase away any animal that comes too close. By the next spring, the young swans are ready to live on their own.

SWAN SUCCESS

In the wild, swans can live for more than 20 years — some even reach 30!

Plunk! A young trumpeter swan drops into a safe, clean marsh.

Long ago, trumpeter swans almost disappeared. People hunted them for their feathers and skin. By 1933, fewer than 70 were left in the whole United States.

Then people worked hard to help them. Laws stopped the hunting. Safe places were set aside just for swans. Slowly, their numbers grew year after year.

Today, there are over 60,000 trumpeter swans! Other swans need help, too. Keeping lakes and rivers clean is important because swans need healthy water to live and raise their families.

SPOT SWANS

Winter is the best time to see huge flocks of swans — some lakes have thousands!

Rustle! A child peeks through the reeds and spots a swan!

You can find swans at many parks and nature areas. Look for them on calm lakes, ponds, and rivers. Early morning is the best time to spot them feeding.

Bring a pair of binoculars if you can. Stay quiet and move slowly. Swans may swim closer if you sit still and wait patiently.

Never chase or feed wild swans. Keep a safe distance, about 30 feet away. Watch how they dip, glide, and care for their young. These graceful birds will make your visit unforgettable!

GLOSSARY

waterfowl

A bird that lives on or near water

webbed

Having skin that connects the toes

preening

Cleaning and fixing feathers with the beak

cygnet

A baby swan

bevy

A group of swans on the water